Flight

Chris Oxlade

KINGFISHER
NEW YORK

KINGFISHER
LONDON & NEW YORK

Copyright © Kingfisher 2012
Published in the United States by Kingfisher,
175 Fifth Ave., New York, NY 10010
Kingfisher is an imprint of Macmillan Children's Books, London.
All rights reserved.

Distributed in the U.S. and Canada by Macmillan,
175 Fifth Ave., New York, NY 10010

Library of Congress Cataloging-in-Publication data
has been applied for.

Series editor: Thea Feldman
Literacy consultant: Ellie Costa, Bank St. College, New York
Flight consultant: Andrew Nahun
Text for U.S. edition written by Thea Feldman

ISBN: 978-0-7534-6881-4 (HB)
ISBN: 978-0-7534-6882-1 (PB)

Kingfisher books are available for special promotions
and premiums. For details contact: Special Markets
Department, Macmillan, 175 Fifth Ave.,
New York, NY 10010.

For more information, please visit
www.kingfisherbooks.com

Printed in China
9 8 7 6 5 4 3 2 1
1TR/0712/UG/WKT/105MA

Picture credits
The Publisher would like to thank the following for permission to reproduce their material. Every care has
been taken to trace copyright holders. However, if there have been unintentional omissions or failure to trac
copyright holders, we apologize and will, if informed, endeavor to make corrections in any future edition
(t = top, c = center, r = right, l = left):
Cover Shutterstock/Takahashi Photography; Shutterstock/David Brimm; Pages 4–5 Photolibrary/age foto;
5t Shutterstock/MarchCattle; 5b Shutterstock/Mircea Bezergheanu; 6 Photolibrary/corbis; 7 Shutterstock/
IDesign; 8t Frank Lane Picture Agency (FLPA)/Jef Meul; 8b Alamy/WaterFrame; 9 FLPA/Michael Durham/
Minden; 10 Alamy/MEPL; 11t Alamy/The Art Archive; 12 Science Photo Libraru (SPL)/Science Source;
13t Alamy/Todd Muskopf; 13b SPL/US Library of Congress; 15 Shutterstock/Ivan Cholakov Gostock-dot-ne
16 Shutterstock/Paul Drabot; 17b Shutterstock/Ramon Berk; 18 Shutterstock/Carlos E. Santa Maria;
19b Shutterstock/Oleg Yarko; 20 Alamy/Nick Servian; 21t Photolibrary/Corbis; 21b Alamy/Antony Nettle;
22 Shutterstock/Yves Smolders; 23t Shutterstock/Gabriel Nardelli Araujo; 23b Alamy/Andi Duff;
24 Shutterstock/David Brimm; 26 Shutterstock/Uwe Bumann; 27t Shutterstock/Gary Blakeley; 27b Corbis;
Photolibrary/Pure Stock; 29 Corbis; all other images from the Kingfisher Artbank.

Contents

Flight and flying

What do birds, planes, and kites have in common? They all fly! Flying, or the act of flight, means to travel through the air. All sorts of things fly, from butterflies to helicopters to rockets.

Birds fly to find food for themselves and their young. They also take off to escape from predators such as foxes.

plane taking off

Kites

A kite is a very simple flying machine. Wind lifts a kite into the air. You control a kite by using the string attached to its end, or tail.

Birds in flight

Birds make flying look easy. And, for them, it is! A bird flies with its wings. The wings have a curved shape. When a bird flies, air goes over and under the wings. This lifts the bird into the air. Bird wings are covered with special feathers called flight feathers.

Bones: A bird's bones are very strong, but they are also very light.

Muscles: A bird has strong muscles that move its wings.

Tail: A bird uses the feathers on its tail to steer and to slow dow

Did you know?

The albatross has the longest wings of any bird. Th distance from the tip of one wing to the tip of the other wing can be 11 feet (3.4 meters) long—that's the same length as two adults lying head to toe.

This tiny hummingbird flaps its wings so fast that the wings make a humming noise. It is drinking nectar from a flower.

Wings on the move

Small birds, such as starlings and robins, flap their wings fast to keep flying. Bigger birds, like eagles and gulls, **glide** a lot. They fly with wings spread out wide.

More flying animals

Bees, flies, butterflies, and dragonflies are all insects that fly. Insects fly to look for food. Small flying insects, such as bees and wasps, flap their tiny wings very fast. Their flapping wings make the buzzing sound you hear when they fly near you.

Can fish fly?

Not really. But flying fish are named for the way they leap out of the water, spread their fins, and glide through the air.

s are mammals with wings. Most bats are
turnal. This means they sleep in the
time and fly at night. Bats make sounds as
y fly, and they listen for the sounds to
nce back off things. The sounds that come
k tell bats where things are. This is how bats
food, such as moths. Humans can't hear
sounds that bats make.

e skin on a bat's wing
tretched between its
g fingers.

Trying to fly

People wanted to fly a long time before **aircraft** were invented. They saw birds flying by and wanted to copy them. But they didn't know how birds flew.

Some people made wings that looked like bird wings. They put them on their arms and jumped from tall towers. But people were not able to fly this way. They needed to build flying machines.

The story of Icarus

In a story from ancient Greece, a boy named Icarus flew with wings made of wax and feathers. But when he flew too close to the Sun, the wax melted and Icarus fell to Earth.

The first time people flew was in a balloon, in the year 1783. Two French brothers named Montgolfier made the balloon. Fire was used to heat the air inside the balloon. Hot air rises and the hot air made the balloon float up.

The Montgolfiers' balloon was made from paper and was brightly painted.

In 1890, a French inventor named Clement Ader built a plane that looked like a box with giant bat wings. It had a steam engine and a giant **propeller**.

Clement Ader's plane only managed to go about 165 feet (50 meters).

11

The first plane

In 1903, a plane with an engine flew into the air for the first time. The plane was called *Flyer*. It was built by two American brothers, Wilbur and Orville Wright.

Orville Wright at the controls of one of the Wright brothers' planes

Before they built *Flyer*, the Wright brothers did a lot of experiments with kites and **gliders**. They figured out how to make wings and how to make a plane go up and come down. They learned how to make a plane turn left or right too.

Elevator: This made *Flyer* go up or come down.

Wings: *Flyer* was a **biplane**, which means it had two pairs of wings. The end of the wings would move to make the plane turn left or right.

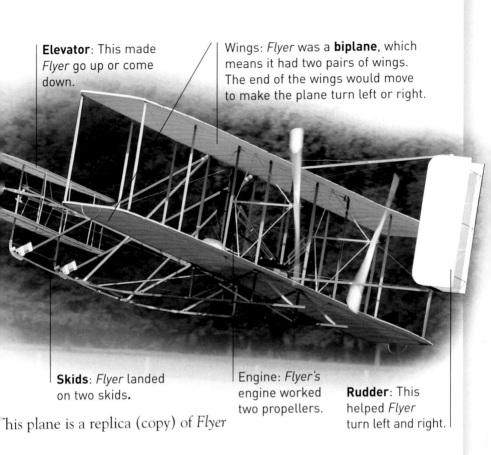

Skids: *Flyer* landed on two skids.

Engine: *Flyer's* engine worked two propellers.

Rudder: This helped *Flyer* turn left and right.

This plane is a replica (copy) of *Flyer*

famous flight

Orville Wright was the pilot when *Flyer* took off for the first time. His brother Wilbur held his breath as he watched *Flyer* speed along the ground and rise into the air. The flight only lasted a few seconds, but *Flyer* worked!

13

Modern planes

Modern planes look very different from the planes the Wright brothers flew. The body of a plane is called the **fuselage** (say "foo-sih-loj"). The fuselage is shaped like a long tube and is made of metal. Passengers or cargo go in the fuselage. The pilot sits in the **cockpit**, which is at the front of the fuselage.

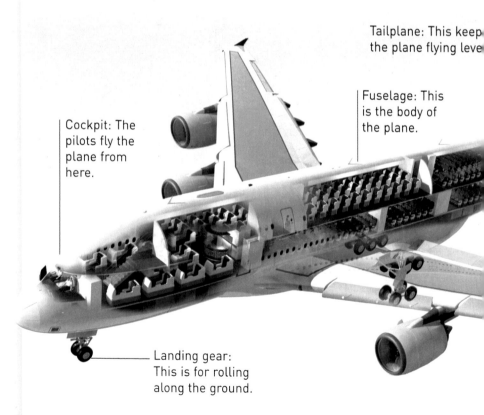

Tailplane: This keeps the plane flying level.

Fuselage: This is the body of the plane.

Cockpit: The pilots fly the plane from here.

Landing gear: This is for rolling along the ground.

Flying forces

This picture shows the pushes and pulls on a plane when it is flying. These pushes and pulls are called forces.

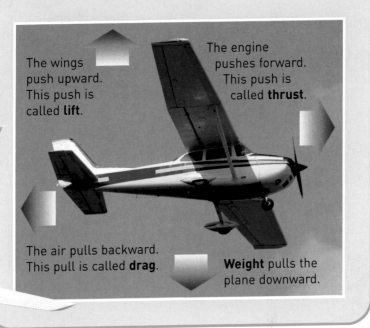

The wings push upward. This push is called **lift**.

The engine pushes forward. This push is called **thrust**.

The air pulls backward. This pull is called **drag**.

Weight pulls the plane downward.

Fin: This keeps the plane flying in a straight line.

Wings: These lift the plane into the air. They only work when the plane is traveling fast enough. If a plane flies too slowly, the wings stop lifting it.

Engine: This pushes the plane through the air.

Plane engines

Engines push planes along. Small planes and slow planes have propeller engines. These engines make a propeller spin very fast, like a giant fan. The propeller pushes on the air, which pushes the plane along.

Most large planes and very fast planes have **jet** engines. These engines don't have propellers. They make a fast stream or jet of gas instead.

You can see the **exhaust** from this fighter plane's two jet engines.

Inside a jet engine, spinning blades squeeze the air. Then the air is mixed with fuel. The fuel burns. This makes a lot of hot gas, which comes out of the engine's exhaust pipe. The gas shoots backward and pushes the plane forward.

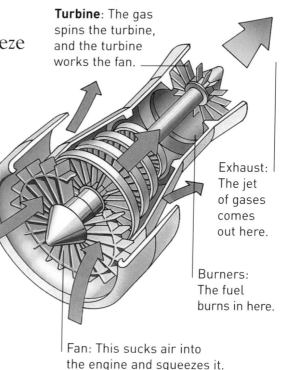

Turbine: The gas spins the turbine, and the turbine works the fan.

Exhaust: The jet of gases comes out here.

Burners: The fuel burns in here.

Fan: This sucks air into the engine and squeezes it.

Did you know?

The biggest jet engine ever made is the General Electric GE90. Its fan is 10.6 feet (3.25 meters) across. The engine was built for an airliner called the Boeing 777. There are two of these engines on each Boeing 777.

Flying a plane

Inside the cockpit the pilot uses **controls** to fly the plane. These include handles, switches, and dials. The controls make the plane go up, down, to the left, and to the right. They help the pilot keep the plane steady and level as it moves through the air. A handle called the **throttle** makes the engines go faster or slower.

Steering a plane

A pilot steers with a stick called the control column
and with two pedals. The control column looks a bit
like a car's steering wheel.

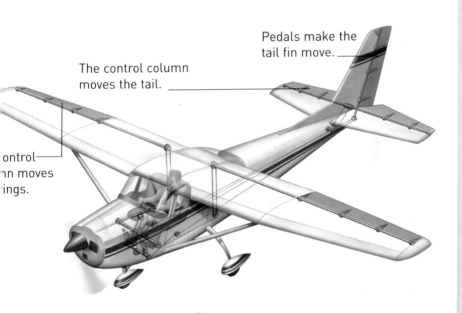

Pedals make the
tail fin move.

The control column
moves the tail.

ontrol
n moves
ings.

Planes with no pilots

Many planes have an
autopilot. This is a
computer that flies a
plane so the pilot can rest.

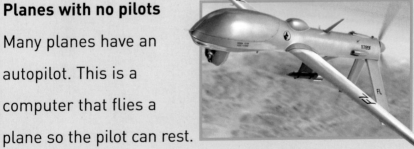

A **spy plane**, like this one, doesn't have a pilot at all.
People on the ground fly it, using remote controls.

19

Takeoff and landing

Takeoff is when a plane lifts off the ground.
Planes take off from a long, flat strip called a
runway. A pilot steers the plane down the
runway. He or she puts the engines on full
power and the plane moves forward. It moves
faster and faster until it lifts into the air.

A plane must move very fast in order
to take off.

This plane is about to land.

At the end of a flight, a plane lands on another runway. This is the most difficult part of a flight for the pilot. The pilot slows down the plane and lowers the **landing gear**. As soon as the plane's wheels touch the runway, the engines are put into reverse. This quickly stops the plane.

Going straight up

Some planes don't need runways because when they take off, they go straight up! In these kinds of planes, the exhaust pipes point down. The force of the exhaust

sends the plane, like this F-35 fighter plane, into the air. These planes can take off from a ship's deck.

Gliders

A glider is a plane that doesn't have engines. Gliders need help to take off. A plane with an engine tows a glider into the air on a long rope. When the glider is high up, the plane lets it go. Then the glider glides gently back to the ground.

A glider has long, thin wings, which help it stay in the air for as long as it can.

This is a paraglider. The pilot pulls the strings to steer.

ome gliders don't look like planes at all. hang glider has just a wing. The pilot hangs nderneath. A paraglider looks like a kite or a arachute. The kite fills with air as it flies along.

Gliding in a suit

This **skydiver** is wearing a gliding suit. It has small wings on each side. The skydiver spreads his arms and legs to glide down through the air.

Helicopters

Do you hear something noisy in the sky? It may be a helicopter. The noise comes from the helipcoter's **rotor**. The rotor spins very fast and lifts the helicopter into the air. A helicopter doesn't need a runway to take off or land. Its rotor takes it straight up and then straight down.

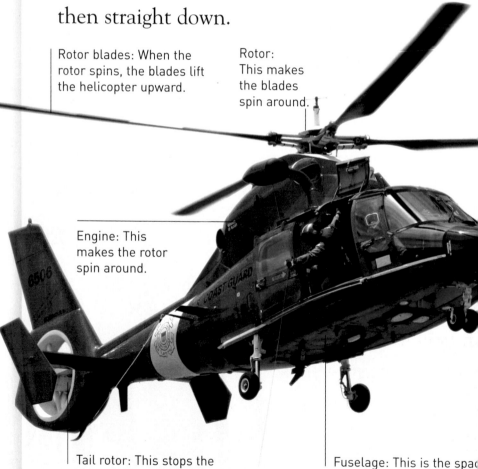

Rotor blades: When the rotor spins, the blades lift the helicopter upward.

Rotor: This makes the blades spin around.

Engine: This makes the rotor spin around.

Tail rotor: This stops the fuselage from spinning around.

Fuselage: This is the space for passengers and cargo.

This rescue
helicopter is lifting
a man from the sea.

Did you know?

The biggest helicopter ever made was called the Mil V-12 and it was made in the 1960s. It had two giant rotors side by side and could carry 90,000 pounds (40 metric tonnes) of cargo.

A helicopter can go where other flying machines cannot. A passenger helicopter can land in a small space in the city. It can even land on the top of a building. A helicopter can also stay still and stay in the air. That makes it able to help rescue people from the sea or the mountains.

Jobs planes do

Planes do lots of different jobs. Most planes are passenger planes. Large passenger planes carry hundreds of people for thousands of miles without stopping. Cargo planes carry things from place to place. Inside a cargo plane's fuselage is a huge empty space, ready to be filled with goods, packages, and parcels.

Workers loading
a cargo plane

Did you know?

The biggest airliner in the world is the Airbus A380. It is a double-decker plane and is 240 feet (73 meters) long. It can carry 853 passengers.

his fire-fighting plane is
opping a load of water.

ome planes do special jobs. There are
anes that fight forest fires and planes
at work as flying ambulances. Some
anes carry fuel for other planes, and
me planes are used to spray crops.

A fighter plane getting
fuel from a tanker plane

Space flight

Three . . . two . . . one . . . Liftoff!
Rockets carry astronauts and cargo into space.

A rocket has an engine that pushes it upward

and into space. Fuel burns inside the engine and makes hot gases. The gases blast out of the engine and push the rocket upward.

After liftoff, the rocket goes faster and faster. After a few minutes it starts to fly around Earth.

SpaceShipTwo is a new spacecraft that will carry tourists into space. It is lifted into the air by *WhiteKnightTwo*, a jet plane with two fuselages. The spacecraft is released and it flies in space for a few minutes. Then it glides back to Earth.

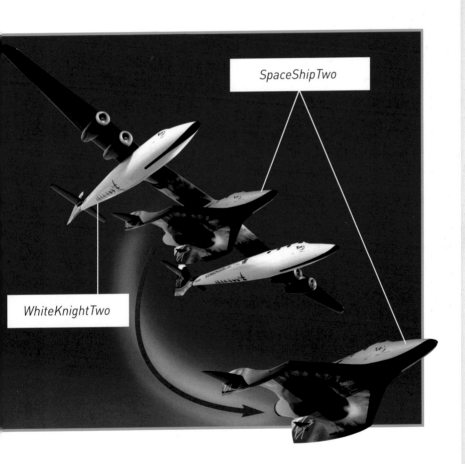

SpaceShipTwo

WhiteKnightTwo

This picture shows *SpaceShipTwo* leaving *WhiteKnightTwo* on its way to space.

Glossary

aircraft a machine that flies

biplane a plane with two pairs of wings

cockpit the space in a plane where the pilot sits

controls things in the cockpit, such as handles, switches, pedals, and dials that a pilot uses to fly a plane

drag a push from the air that slows down a plane

elevator the part on the tail of a plane that helps the plane go up or down

exhaust gases that come out of an engine

fuselage the body of a plane, shaped like a tube

glide to fly without moving wings (bird) or without using an engine (plane)

glider a plane with no engine

jet a fast-moving stream of gases

landing gear aircraft wheels used for landing, takeoff, and moving on the ground

lift an upward push made by a plane's wing

propeller an object

...ke a fan that is turned
...y a plane's engine and
...ushes a plane along

...tor part of a flying
...achine that spins
...ound very fast

...dder the part that
...elps some planes, like
...he *Flyer*, turn left or
...ght

...nway a long, flat
...rip of land where
...anes take off and
...nd

...ids a part on some
...f the first airplanes
...n which the plane
...nded

...ydiver a person who
...mps from a plane and
...nds using a parachute

...y plane a plane that

flies high in the sky
and photographs the
ground below

throttle a handle that
the pilot uses to make
a plane go faster or
slower

thrust the push made
by a plane's engines

turbine a part of a
plane that keeps
turning and helps a
plane move forward

weight the pull made
by gravity that makes
things fall to the
ground

Index